Ripley's—

BRUTAL BEASTS

Believe It or Not!®

Ripley
PUBLISHING
a Jim Pattison Company

Written by Camilla de la Bedoyere
Consultant Barbara Taylor

Ripley
PUBLISHING

Publisher Anne Marshall

Editorial Director Rebecca Miles
Project Editor Charlotte Howell
Picture Researchers Michelle Foster,
Charlotte Howell
Proofreader Lisa Regan
Indexer Hilary Bird

Art Director Sam South
Senior Designer Michelle Foster
Design Rocket Design (East Anglia) Ltd
Reprographics Juice Creative Ltd

www.ripleybooks.com

ISBN 978-1-60991-084-6
10 9 8 7 6 5 4 3 2 1

For information regarding permission, write to VP
Intellectual Property, Ripley Entertainment Inc., Suite 188,
7576 Kingspointe Parkway, Orlando, Florida 32819
email: publishing@ripleys.com
Library of Congress Cataloging-in-Publication Data
is available.
Printed in China
in June/2013
1st printing

PUBLISHER'S NOTE
While every effort has been made to verify the accuracy
of the entries in this book, the Publishers cannot be held
responsible for any errors contained in the work. They
would be glad to receive any information from readers.

WARNING
Some of the stunts and activities in this book are
undertaken by experts and should not be attempted by
anyone without adequate training and supervision.

CONTENTS

PAGE 19

27

34

NATURE'S NASTIES

DEADLY PERILS AND HIDDEN HAZARDS

Nature is mostly nasty, not nice. Every animal on our planet has to fight to survive—and the fight is often to the death. Beasts have to be brutal: that means they need killing skills, lethal weapons, and cruel cunning.

This is no ordinary nature trek. Ripley's will take you through jungles, swamps, and creeks. We will explore the dangers that lurk in the deepest seas and in the darkest hideaways, where deadly animals prowl. There are many perils in store, and hidden hazards at every twist and turn. Are you ready for the terrifying trip of a lifetime?

fast on her feet

can live almost anywhere

quiet and stealthy

enormous fangs

She-devil

Stand back—this leopard is a prima donna and doesn't like having her photo taken. She's brutal and she knows it—that's one baaaad attitude.

CREEPIEST DESERT CENTIPEDE

11

A creepy-crawly with lots of legs and big jaws.

CRUNCHIEST PRAYING MANTIS

14

A bug that crunches its prey with jackknife claws.

BEASTLY EXTREMES!

This snake has two heads! Most snakes like this don't live very long—except for one two-headed rat snake with two stomachs and two throats that lived for 20 years!

These books are about "Believe It or Not!"—amazing facts, feats, and things that make you go "Wow!"

KEY FACTS

Read more unbelievable facts when you spot a Key Facts box.

Look out for the "Twist It" column on some pages. Twist the book to find out more amazing facts about brutal beasts.

PACKING PUNCHES

EXPLOSIVE POWER

It's a big, bad, brutal, and savage world out there. Could you ever imagine exploding ants, kangaroos that box, or beetles that squirt chemicals from their butt?

Whether they are packing a powerful punch or mixing up chemicals to make a bomb, these cruel critters are truly awesome. They can use excessive force to get their own way, so stand back and watch these animal antics!

WANNA FIGHT?

Ding ding, round one, and the kangaroo in the blue corner is swinging at the kangaroo in the red corner. Over on the Australian grassland there are two kangaroos battling it out in the boxing ring. It's turning nasty and someone's going to get hurt!

Male kangaroos—boomers—get dirty when they fight over a female. They kick out with their massive feet and box with their sharply clawed paws. They are strong enough to crush bone!

BIG WORD ALERT
MARSUPIAL
say mar-soo-pi-al
An animal that looks after its baby in a pouch.

Taking one for the team

This little carpenter ant has given up its life to save the lives of the ants it lives with. When a bigger ant from another nest attacked its home, the carpenter ant exploded its own body, producing toxic yellow glue that killed them both.

Super spit

Spitting cobras can fire blinding venom with a deadly aim. They target their victim's eyes and are accurate 90 percent of the time, even when the victim is moving.

A hot shot

This little beetle fears no one because it knows it can fight back using an explosion in its bottom! It keeps two chemicals stashed away near its tail, and when the moment is right they are allowed to mix. The potion gets really hot and explodes, forcing a foul-smelling liquid to spray in the direction of an attacker. Impressive!

TWIST IT!

Jellyfish can fire their poisoned barbs in under one-millionth of a second!

Never anger a llama—these feisty animals have short tempers and are quick to kick, head-butt, and bite. Freaked-out males also shoot out big gobbets of spit at an enemy!

Ural owls hate to see anyone near their chicks and they lash out with their huge talons, delivering a punch that can knock a man off his feet.

TAKE COVER!

Finding clams is tricky when the crunchy-shelled critters hide in soft mud. Walruses solve the problem by squirting a jet of water to remove the mud, leaving the clams exposed and ready to eat!

Found a new word? Big Word Alert will explain it for you.

QUICKEST PEREGRINE FALCON
23
Swift in the air and the world's fastest killer.

BLOODIEST SHORT-HORNED LIZARD
34
A scary face—and it can ooze blood from its eyes.

STINKIEST SKUNK
35
Squirts a stench bad enough to make you vomit.

NASTIEST MARINE WORM
36
So gross we weren't sure we could even show you this one!

PACK POWER

GRUESOME GANGS GRAB THE BIG PRIZES

Hard-working hunters can make life easier by pulling together. One lion may have some success at catching a buffalo, but just imagine how powerful a whole pack of predators can be.

Working as a team isn't easy. Every animal must understand the plan of attack, and know what its job is. Not all animals can pull together like this—it takes cool cunning and brains.

African wild dogs are also known as painted dogs because of their strange multi-colored fur.

TOP DOGS

Your pet pooch may seem cute and cuddly, but tame dogs are closely related to wild and brutal beasts, such as wolves, coyotes, dingos, and African wild dogs. They belong to one big animal family called "canids." Canids often live in family groups, and hunt together as a pack. With their incredible sense of smell and great eyesight, canids can detect their prey from far away.

African wild dogs don't waste their time creeping up on their prey. The pack simply chooses a target then chases it until it collapses. They can eat through bone and, when they are full, they regurgitate some food (bring it up from their stomach) to share with relatives that were too weak to take part in the chase.

Hunting hawks

Most birds of prey prefer to go solo when hunting, but Harris hawks have found they get to eat more often when they work together as a family. They surround a rabbit, and when it starts to run the bird closest swoops down for the kill, and the meal is shared between the team.

BIG WORD ALERT
PREDATOR
An animal that kills other animals (prey) to eat.

Hunting in a pack, wolves can attack prey that is up to ten times the size of any one member of the team.

TWIST IT!

When dolphins spy a group of fish, one dolphin swiftly swims in a big circle around the fish. This stirs up mud and sand so the fish have to turn back—and straight into waiting jaws.

Lions have huge teeth for stabbing and slicing food, but they can't chew.

A male adult lion can eat 75 pounds of meat in one sitting—that's 300 quarter pounders!

Lions often hunt at night, and they are most successful when there's no moon. Like all cats, they can see even when there is very little light, but their prey can't.

Hyenas are dog-like pack hunters of the African grasslands. They look, and act, like dogs but they are more closely related to cats!

THE BRAT PACK

The big bad wolf

There's a reason grey wolves are the bad guys in children's stories—they really are cunning creatures that are happy to see Little Red Riding Hood on the menu! Wolf attacks used to be quite common in parts of Europe and North America. Nowadays, wolves are rare and they hunt deer, oxen, and moose instead of humans—phew!

Ripley's Believe It or Not!®

Big-cat keeper Riana van Nieuwenhuizen, from South Africa, shares her house with nine cheetahs, three leopards, two wolves, a jaguar, a lion, and three dogs! She looks after the orphaned animals from birth and hopes to raise awareness of endangered species in her country.

Taking pride in your work

Hunting is a family affair for lions. A pride (family group) is mostly made up of females and their cubs, and it's the ladies who lunch— or at least go and get lunch! These clever cats have different tricks for catching their prey, but one cunning plan is this simple:

1. One female walks up to a grazing buffalo.

2. The buffalo is spooked, and runs away in the opposite direction.

3. Other lionesses are ready and waiting—they are hiding just where the buffalo is heading.

4. The buffalo gets a nasty shock when it sees a handful of lions bounding toward it. There's no escape...

BRUTE STRENGTH

ANIMAL CHAMPS
WITH MIGHTY MUSCLES

It's time to get out the big guns—and show those muscles! Strength can be a top factor in survival so these animals have grown large and strong. When battle begins, there can only be one winner.

Join muscles to bones and you create an impressive bit of engineering—and the power to do some deadly damage to your enemy. Add a fearless attitude, and you've created a killing machine.

BRUTAL BEASTS

BEWARE OF DRAGONS

Dinosaurs are long-dead, but beware these reminders of a bygone time! A Komodo dragon wouldn't look out of place in a prehistoric forest and it has a furious temper to match that fierce face. In fact, these brutal beasts are so nasty their babies have to hide in trees to keep out of harm's way—the parents sometimes turn cannibal!

Max size: 10 feet long

Mega fact: The world's largest lizards, Komodos eat anything they can catch—including humans.

KEY FACTS

MEGA-MONSTERS OF LONG AGO

Enormous beasts ruled the world millions of years ago. Check out some of these super-sized brutes:

Titanoboa
The largest snake that ever lived ruled the rainforests after the dinosaurs died out. It was as long as a *T. rex* and its body was as thick as a human waist.

Pristichampsus
How scary would it be if a crocodile could stand up on its back legs and run after you? Be glad you weren't around about 50 million years ago, with this giant croc-like creature!

Megaspiders
Long ago, giant spiders were common. There was more oxygen in the air, which meant breathing was easier, and all sorts of bugs and spiders could grow bigger.

Brontoscorpio
Scientists have found evidence of a mighty scorpion that lived in the water and grew to 3 feet long.

Ripley's Believe It or Not!®
Tigers in the Sundarbans mangrove forests in India and Bangladesh often attack humans from behind. So local fisherman came up with a way to prevent the attacks—by wearing masks on the back of their heads so the tigers think they are facing them.

BRUTAL BEASTS

SILENT BUT DEADLY

This is one of the world's most powerful killers. It may look gorgeous but only a fool would mess with a tiger. With a reputation for attacking grown men, tigers are scared of nothing and no one. They are strong, silent, and very, very deadly.

Max size: 11 feet nose to tail

Mega fact: About 100 years ago, the Champawat tigress killed more than 400 people in India and Nepal.

BRUTAL BEASTS

OH DEAR, DEER!

Enormous wings, big bills, and terrifying talons—golden eagles are North America's largest birds of prey with the killing skills to think big. They mainly hunt rabbits, lizards, and even insects—but sometimes their eyes are bigger than their stomach, and eagles swoop to attack deer. This deer had a lucky escape when it dived under a fence.

Max size: 7 feet 6 inch wingspan

Mega fact: Golden eagles can dive-bomb their prey, reaching speeds of 150 mph.

BRUTAL BEASTS

TURNING THE TABLE

Birds love to eat wriggling spiders, swallowing them whole—but this bird got a bit of a shock! Goliath bird-eating spiders are big enough to turn the tables and can catch small birds. Most of the time, they settle for a snack of frogs, lizards, beetles, or mice.

Max size: 11 inch legspan

Mega fact: The spider's fangs are longer than a human fingernail and deliver a nasty dose of poison.

BRUTAL BEASTS

BEAR-FACED GREEDY-GUTS

Fruit, berries, and roots keep a grizzly bear happy, but their giant cousins, polar bears, are definitely not vegetarians! These meat-lovers live where it's too cold for plants to grow so they have to feast on flesh. Seals are usually on the menu and it takes the bear's huge strength and size, massive paws, and ferocious fangs to kill one.

Max size: 8 feet 6 inches nose to tail

Mega fact: A large polar bear was stuffed and put on display at Anchorage Airport in Alaska. It stands over 7 feet tall.

LETHAL INJECTION

GETTING STRAIGHT TO THE POINT

Is it possible to be brutal and a weakling? These animals may not have large bodies, brute strength, or big brains, but they don't need any of those things. They have a super scary secret up their sleeves.

It's VENOM! A poisonous liquid that is injected straight into the body and has a range of nasty effects. Venom can cause severe pain, make flesh rot and die, stop victims from breathing or moving, or make them bleed to death… the list just goes on and on!

Freaky fangs

It is this spider's attitude that makes it so dangerous, not just its venom. When male Sydney funnel web spiders are in the mood for love they leave their burrows and embark on a search for a lady-friend—and they won't let anything get in their way. Anyone in their path is likely to get a nasty nip with those fearsome fangs—and their venom is one of the most deadly known.

KEY FACTS

The world's top five venomous snakes all live in Australia. These snakes have the most deadly venom, but some of them are very short-tempered.

* 1. Inland taipan
* 2. Eastern brown snake
* 3. Coastal taipan
* 4. Tiger snake
* 5. Black tiger snake

Inland taipan snake

BIG WORD ALERT

VENOM

Poisonous liquid that is injected into a victim's body.

Spider slayer

This incredible insect has an unbelievable—and totally revolting—life story. It's a tarantula hawk wasp and it is attacking an enormous tarantula, spider, which it grabs with its claws, then stings. The wasp will take the sleepy spider back to its burrow and lay an egg inside its body. When the egg hatches, the larva (young insect) will devour the still-living spider from the inside out!

Tail bends over the head. **2**

Tip of the tail injects venom into victim's body. **3**

A sting in the tail

Scorpions love to hide in small dark places, so wise desert campers always check their shoes in the morning! A scorpion sting can be very painful, and one from a deathstalker scorpion can be fatal to children.

Strong jaws mash the victim's body into a pulp. **4**

1 Big claws grab prey.

ACTUAL SIZE

Lethal legs

The giant desert centipede can grow up to 8 inches long! It uses its maxillipeds—which literally means "jaw-feet"—to grab hold of prey and inject venom into its body.

TWIST IT!

VENOMONSTERS

There are about 3,000 types of snake in the world, and around 300 of these are dangerous to humans.

Venomous lizards, such as gila monsters, use their teeth for injecting venom, chewing, and munching to force the venom deeper into flesh.

There are two types of shark that are known to have venomous spines: Port Jackson sharks and spiny dogfish (also known as spurdogs).

There are no venomous birds, but there are a few birds that have poisonous skin and feathers.

11

FEARLESS FIENDS

THE RIPLEY HALL OF HEROES

All around the world, nations give medals and awards to people who have shown great courage or skill in battle. We believe there is no reason to leave animals out—many of these creatures show incredible bravery and will fight to the death.

We take great pleasure in announcing the following awards to the brutal beasts of the animal kingdom.

AWARDED FOR:
GREAT SKILL AND DARING DEFENSE OF THE SKIES

RIPLEY'S AWARD FOR FLYING COMBAT

The Award is given to goshawks, secretive birds of prey that defend their nests against all intruders.

Goshawks are fearless fliers and will dive-bomb any animal that enters their own space, or territory. They are plucky birds, and will attack animals much bigger than themselves, including bears and wolves. These raptors don't flinch from danger, and will even launch an attack on humans.

RIPLEY'S STAR OF COURAGE

The Star is awarded to wolverines because they combine all the qualities of great predators.

Wolverines are about as big as a medium-sized dog, but they compete and hunt for animals that are many times their size. When a wolverine spots an animal it goes in for the kill— it even attacks wolves and black bears with its strong body and clawed-paws.

AWARDED FOR:
FIGHTING BATTLES AGAINST ALL ODDS

Find out even more about this meany on page 40

AWARDED FOR:
FEARLESS ATTITUDE AND GREAT STRENGTH

RIPLEY'S NOBLE ORDER OF THE CLAW

The Order is given to honey badgers, which have a sweet name but are often called "the meanest animals alive."

Honey badgers raid beehives to eat the eggs and larvae, and feast on honey, but they will attack almost any animal that takes their fancy. With their enormous claws and teeth, these stout-hearted predators are able to kill small crocodiles and large or poisonous snakes.

RIPLEY'S MEDAL OF HONOR

The Medal is awarded to all female elephants who have risked life and limb to protect their families.

When a baby elephant is attacked by groups of hyenas or lions, a mother elephant turns her back on fear and faces the pack. Like an out-of-control tank the mother charges the pack, using feet, trunk, and tusks to attack. She puts her baby's life, or that of her sisters' babies, above care for her own safety, and is a shining example to us all.

AWARDED FOR:
RISKING OWN LIFE TO SAVE OTHERS

MIGHTY MAULERS

KILLER LIMBS TO TEAR, RIP, AND MAUL

Paws, claws, jaws, talons, and knife-like limbs—these beasts have got the lot! Serious assassins need the right tools for the job.

When a mighty mauler has its eyes on the prize it needs more than wishful thinking to get lunch in its tum. It has to chase, catch, kill, shred, and slash its prey—with limbs that are perfectly adapted for butchery.

Whipped into a frenzy

This miniature monster is a whip spider. It's part of the scorpion and spider family, but it manages to maul its prey without the use of a venomous bite or sting. Instead, it relies on brute force and two huge barbed front limbs, which can touch, grab, stab, crush, and mash its victims.

When a mantis attacks, it moves so quickly that it's almost impossible to see the movement with the naked ey

Say a prayer

Male praying mantises treat their female mates with great care, but they still often find themselves on the menu. These super-sized bugs are armed with forelegs that work like jackknives with folding blades. Normally, this scissor action is kept for prey, but female mantises often can't resist the urge to kill and eat their unfortunate male mates.

TOOLED UP

Mantises can move their head 180 degrees and they have two big eyes, as well as three smaller ones, which means they can spot anything moving nearby.

Vinegaroons (a type of scorpion) carry their babies on their backs until they are ready to look after themselves. The mothers don't eat, and often die of starvation soon after.

A giant anteater can stick its tongue out more than 2 feet to lick up ants. It can use its huge claws to defend itself against big cats, such as pumas.

Talons are made of keratin—the same stuff that your nails and hair are made of. They keep growing, just like nails, all through a bird's life, but they get worn down with use.

TWIST IT!

Ripley's—— Believe It or Not!

This very odd-looking animal is actually a frog—known as a hairy frog! This amazing creature has retractable claws, made of bone, which it pushes through its skin to defend itself, breaking the bones of its toes as they are forced through.

Digging deep

Anteaters may be toothless, but that doesn't stop them from being one of the world's most effective killers. How many other animals can kill tens of thousands of victims in one day? This anteater is using its claws to dig a hole into a bug nest. It sticks its long tongue into the hole, flicking it three times a second. It can eat up to 30,000 ants in one day.

Mega legs

Secretary birds have very long legs. This bird of prey uses them to stomp through the African grasslands, chasing any little animals that try to run away. The victim is stamped or kicked to death and swallowed whole. Even poisonous snakes are killed this way, as they are too far from the bird's body to get a chance to deliver a deadly bite.

Birds of prey (raptors) use their talons to fight off predators, grasp onto branches and, most importantly, to hold and rip their victims to shreds.

SLAUGHTER IN THE WATER

NATURE'S CRUEL RIVERS

Come on board the Ripley's River Cruise of Cruelty. We've collected together some of the world's meanest animals in one place, so let's go on a journey of deadly discovery.

Don't be fooled by the gently rippling surface— rivers and their surroundings are home to plenty of scary critters. They may be hidden from view, but that's the plan. The most effective predators are ones you don't see until it's too late…

Wow, look at that!

Ladies and gentlemen, boys and girls, look to the river bank and, between the plants and the forest shadows, you'll spy a jaguar. A powerful big cat of the Americas, this predator—with a caiman in its jaws—is the heavyweight of the feline family. Look at that vast, broad head and solid shoulders. This prize-fighter is as happy in the river as it is in the forest.

Argh, look at the teeth on that!

Here's one of the most famous river predators of all time—a piranha! There are 20 species of piranha, but only four are dangerous, especially the red-bellied piranha. Those sharp teeth can do some serious harm!

Woah, he's a beauty!

Just to the side of the boat you will see, curled up among the reeds, a super slithering squeezing beast. Shhh, it's a yellow anaconda and we don't want to scare it. It is hiding there, waiting for a bird, rat, or fish to pounce on. It wraps its coils around its prey, slowly suffocating it to death.

And now, grab your binoculars and zoom in on the water, just by that floating branch. See the giant otter, ripping and tearing into a fish? It's a tough beast with an attitude to match—listen out for it barking, growling, snorting, and screaming! It loves fish, but it also hunts anacondas and caimans.

Quick, over there!

KILLER SKILLS

GLADIATORS OF THE ANIMAL WORLD

She's protecting her baby!

The gladiators of Ancient Rome fought in fierce combat—to the death. They had special training, and an impressive range of skills and weapons. Perhaps they got some of their inspiration from looking at these brutal beasts?

The natural world is full of surprises. Who could ever imagine this amazing range of battle skills and strategies? There is a huge variety of living things and life styles on Earth, and this is known as biodiversity.

Lunge and strike

Brutal beast: Pit viper

Weapon: Venomous fangs

Skill: Detects the heat from prey

Pit vipers are master snakes of combat. They can sense the vibration caused by an animal moving and— even more impressive—they can "see" the heat that it produces. They create "heat pictures" in their brain, which allow them to judge how far away their prey is, and its size—even in darkness. Their weapons are fangs, which deliver a deadly dose of venom.

Dive-bomb

Brutal beast: *Kestrel*

Weapon: *Talons and beak*

Skill: *Super speed and pee detection*

Kestrels prey on small mammals, such as mice and voles. They find them using their sensitive eyes, which can spot the ultraviolet light reflected from the trails of urine (pee) that the mammals make. Once spotted, the mammal must run at full speed to escape before the kestrel swoops down and grabs it with its talons.

It's a trap

Brutal beast: *Net-casting spider*

Weapon: *Strong, sticky silk*

Skill: *Weaving silk into nets and throwing them*

Net-casting spiders find their prey by sensing its movement, both by touch and sight. Their large eyes can sense light better than those of cats and owls! They weave their silk into webs, and ambush their prey, covering them with a web-net stretched between their legs. Once the victim is under the net, the spider relaxes, and the trap is complete.

Take aim, fire!

Brutal beast: *Porcupine*

Weapon: *Barbed spears*

Skill: *Rapid attack under pressure*

A porcupine prepares itself for attack by turning its back on its enemy and raising its quills, which are like hundreds of barbed spears. The quills come away at the slightest touch and dig into flesh—they are almost impossible to remove.

Spit and lick

Brutal beast: *African crested rat*

Weapon: *Toxic spit*

Skill: *Being prepared*

African crested rats are always prepared for a fight. They chew the roots and bark of a poisonous tree to make a toxic spit, which they paste over the fur on their back. If a predator gets close enough to bite the rat, the fight is over—even a small dose can kill.

THE CRUNCH BUNCH

JAWS AND TEETH

There's no ig-gnaw-ing it—sharp teeth and strong jaws can make any animal brutal! Jaws are crushing machines that come with a wide range of sharp daggers, snapping scissors, munching mincers, and mashers.

Teeth are very useful! Animals can use them to grab their prey, keep it still, kill it, and then break it up into tasty bite-sized portions. Fangs, or canines, can grow extra long and sharp for a stabbing move, while other top and bottom teeth fit together like scissor blades to tear flesh apart. Bigger molars, at the back of the mouth, help grind meat into a juicy paste.

Brown bears are some of the most deadly of all land mammals. Although known to attack humans, thankfully brown bears prefer to eat fish, roots, or berries. When salmon swim upriver to breed, hungry bears lie in wait. The fish have to leap to make it through the cascading water, and that's when the bears get lunch!

KEY FACTS

Bears open their mouth wide and wait for the fish to leap in. A quick snap with those mighty jaws, and the fish's journey is over.

GIGANTIC JAWS

Hippos have a deadly reputation, but just how brutal can a grass-eating, lumbering cousin of a pig be? Very! Hippos attack when they feel threatened. Their teeth, or tusks, can grow up to 20 inches long, and can cut a person in half. Male hippos use their giant jaws and teeth to battle one another at mating time.

Tigers have teeth that are as long as your little finger, so imagine how bad their toothache can get! When Mohan, a white tiger from Dreamland in Brisbane, Australia, began to sulk, his keepers knew something was wrong, and called in a brave dentist. Mohan was put to sleep while Dr. Gary Wilson successfully treated the rotten tooth in a two-hour operation.

ONCE BITTEN

A Titan beetle can snap a pencil in half with its mighty jaws—not impressed? Well, it would be like you biting a tree trunk in half. Bet you're impressed now!

Tuataras are tiny lizardlike reptiles from New Zealand. Although they're small, they can bite off a seagull's head in one snap of the jaws—how gross!

Hyenas have one of the most incredible bites of any animal alive. They can crack bones with one crunch, and eat the bones of their prey—which includes huge beasts such as Cape buffalo.

Scientists have recently discovered a new species of giant wasp called a garuda. Its jaws are longer than its legs!

Giant squid have teeth in their tentacles, but sea urchins have teeth on their bottom!

TWIST IT!

HIGH SPEED CHASE

ANIMAL OLYMPICS

Here in the human world, great athletes and sportspeople pit their skills against one another to achieve glory as supreme champions. We'd like to imagine what it would be like at an Animal Olympics!

These athletes don't need coaches, training, or energy drinks. They've already got what it takes—bodies primed for action, a need for speed, and a ruthless attitude.

The triple jump

Sit back and enjoy the spectacle of an all-round sports star as a gentoo penguin does a hop, skip, and a jump, then a spot of tobogganing, followed by record-setting underwater swimming—accelerating up to 22 mph. These athletes also "fly" above the water, leaping through the air to escape jaws of hungry sharks.

The long jump

While human athletes have struggled to beat the world long jump record of 29 feet 4½ inches, snow leopards could take it in an easy stride. In fact, one snow leopard was seen running and leaping across a ditch that was 49 feet wide!

BIG WORD ALERT

ACCELERATE

When an animal increases its speed it accelerates.

OTHER SPEED FIENDS

Sailfish
68 mph

Cheetah
65 mph

The sprint

When it comes to running, six legs are better than two! The Australian tiger beetle is the world's fastest running insect, reaching top speeds of 5.6 mph, that's the same as a human running at 480 mph. It uses its speed to chase other insects, which it also devours in a super-speedy time!

The slither

If animals organized the Olympics there would have to be a race for the slithering snakes—and the black mamba would be the clear favorite. It may not be able to keep up with Usain Bolt, but a mamba can achieve an impressive 12 mph in short bursts.

The swoop

Bats and insects could take part in Olympic flying events—but the birds would probably take a clean sweep of the medals. The champions of speed are peregrine falcons. As they plunge downward in pursuit of prey, falcons can fly at about 124 mph. No other bird comes close to this incredible feat.

Spiny-tailed iguana
35 mph

Brown bear
35 mph

Sea lion
25 mph

CUNNING KILLERS

NATURE'S BRAINIACS

It has surprised scientists how clever so many animals are. More surprising is how long it has taken the human race to appreciate just what marvelous animals we share our planet with!

In the battle to survive, a big brain is bound to be helpful. Smart animals can make tools, communicate with each other to create a hunting party, plan their actions, and even remember where they have been and what they have done.

Er, ROAR!

Mighty mouse

Little grasshopper mice hunt grasshoppers, but they don't like to share. So they scream loudly—making a nasty noise is a good way to keep everyone away! When they come face to face with scorpions, these bright little beasts know they must bite off the scorpions' venomous tail to survive the battle.

Bird brainboxes

Crows, magpies, rooks, and jackdaws are all known to be clever, but Caledonian crows are the brainboxes of the family. They make and use all sorts of tools to get food, such as grubs.

The crows carefully choose twigs, strip bark off them, snap them to the right length, and can even cut them into the perfect shape. The tools are used to pry grubs out of holes, and the crows keep them to use again.

Chimps are champs, not chumps!

Apes and monkeys are our closest cousins, so it's no wonder they are so clever! Most of them eat plants, but chimps love termites and they hunt, too. Like us, chimps can be caring, friendly, and loving but they can sometimes turn violent.

KEY FACTS

DID YOU KNOW?

TWIST IT!

Tiny tarsiers are primates that scuttle through forests at night, hunting bugs. When they get scared, tarsiers call out and their friends come running to their aid. Together they mob the attacker until it turns tail and leaves. Helping out a buddy is a cunning plan, because the favor may be returned one day.

Spotted hyenas live and work in families, and that takes intelligence. The cubs are ruthless, too—usually they are born as twins but sometimes one will kill its twin to get all of its mother's milk!

Aye-ayes are peculiar little primates that eat burrowing grubs from inside tree trunks. It takes a lot of brainpower to figure out how to reach the grubs, so aye-ayes have huge brains for their little bodies.

Egyptian eagles drop stones onto ostrich eggs to smash them open.

BRAIN WAVES

You lookin' at me?

Angry ape!

Big daddy gorillas are a force to be reckoned with when they are angry. But they would rather not get into a brawl, so they stand tall, beat their chest, and roar. It's a smart move that avoids violence.

SMALL BUT MIGHTY

SIZE DOESN'T MATTER

Insects may be annoying, but are they really deadly? If you take the time to watch insects going about their daily lives you will be amazed by just how surprising—and brutal—many of these little animals are.

Insects have just three pairs of legs, but some unbelievable life stories. There are far more insects than there are people on Earth, and we may share our planet with more than five million different types, from beetles to flies, wasps, and butterflies.

No way!

Face invaders

This is one of the most disgusting animal stories you are ever likely to read. Prepare yourself for a gross factor of ten!

Frogs eat bugs, but this bug—called an epomis larva—has got its own back. It has massive jaws and it waves them around when it sees a frog. The frog thinks it's spied something tasty, and rushes over to eat it. The larva leaps up to the frog's throat and digs in with its enormous hooked jaws. Then it feeds on the frog, sucking blood and chomping away on flesh.

If the frog gets "lucky" and manages to eat the larva, it soon regrets its decision and vomits it out—because the larva starts to eat the frog from the inside instead!

Argh! Get it off!

KEY FACTS — BUGS AT WAR

Forget bombs, tanks, missiles, and big guns—for thousands of years war-makers have been using insects to wage war! Believe it or not . . .

* There are plans to put computer chips into caterpillars so when they turn into butterflies they can be used to fly into enemy areas and spy.

* The ancient Romans used catapults to hurl beehives over city walls.

* During World War Two, Japanese bombs were packed with fleas that carried bubonic plague—a foul disease that killed millions of people in the Middle Ages.

KILLER ANTS!

One ant is no big deal, but when an army of ants goes on the march it's a different matter. Working together, ants can build giant nests, collect food, and attack prey much bigger than themselves.

FIRE ANTS

Fire ants love to chew on electrical wires, devour crops, and attack creatures such as grasshoppers and birds. Their sting is so painful it's been compared to an electric shock.

DRIVER ANTS

Driver ants march in swarms of up to 22 million and destroy everything in their path, including snakes and rats.

Bullet ants sting with a poison that causes pain that lasts for hours, and reduces a human victim to tears of agony.

BULLET ANTS

Find out even more about this nasty ant on page 41

LITTLE DEVILS

Hornets are large stinging wasps that use their stings to kill prey and defend themselves from attack by other animals. A swarm of 30 giant Asian hornets can kill 30,000 honey bees in just a few hours.

Lonomia are killer caterpillars with poisonous spines. If touched, the spines break and inject poisons that can be strong enough to kill a human.

In the past, human hunters often tipped their spears and arrows with a paste made from poisonous beetles or caterpillars.

Coo-eee!

These head markings look like two big eyes.

Acid is sprayed from the throat.

Two flashy "tails" grow out of the body after two molts.

Spray that again!

This charming creature gets full marks for its gorgeous looks. It's the caterpillar of a puss moth, and this fancy outfit certainly grabs attention. The weird colors and marks probably tell a predator to stay away, but if the message is missed there's a nasty surprise in store—the caterpillar can spray burning acid at any attacker!

SNEAKERS AND CREEPERS

LOOK OUT, THERE'S DANGER ABOUT!

There is a nasty shock in store—predators use some sneaky tricks to get close enough to attack. Their victims happily go about their business with no idea that a deadly danger lurks nearby.

These savage brutes are out to deceive. Their beastly tricks rely on sneaking, creeping, hiding, faking, and tempting their victims to come close.

Crawl and catch

The Amazonian giant centipede can catch and eat bats! An adult centipede can reach up to 14 inches in length—that's as long as a man's forearm—and is able to climb cave walls. This centipede caught a passing bat using some of its 46 legs!

Ripley's Believe It or Not!

This species of jumping spider can get up close and personal with ants by pretending to be one of the family. This helps the spider get close to prey, and avoids it being eaten by animals that fear a nasty ant sting.

KEY FACTS

SNEAKY TRICKS SPELL SUCCESS

Stealth Animals creep up on their prey in total silence to gain an element of surprise.

Mimicry Pretending to be another animal or a plant is a smart trick if you want to get close to your prey.

Camouflage Using colors and blending into the background makes you invisible to your victims.

Master of disguise

Look closely at this mossy tree trunk and you will see a leaf-tailed gecko—a type of lizard. This reptile is so well camouflaged even his mother wouldn't recognize him!

TWIST IT!

A tiger's stripes help it to blend into the stripy shadows of its forest home.

Arctic foxes have brown fur in the summer, when there is no snow about, but in the winter their fur turns white so they are perfectly camouflaged.

Glass frogs are virtually transparent (see-through) so they almost disappear when sitting on a leaf.

SEE ME?

Broad and long wings allow the owl to glide, which is quieter than flapping wings.

Swoop and snatch

Snowy owls are white and blend into a white background perfectly. Their feathers are soft and fluffy to deaden the sound as they silently swoop through the air to snatch mice and rats from the ground.

Soft fluffy feathers help to absorb sound.

The ends of these feathers have a special shape. It muffles the noise caused by air passing over them.

Poor mouse doesn't know what's coming!

Stick and slurp

Chameleons are lizards with a long sticky tongue. They can hide amongst the leaves, and shoot out their tongue to grab passing bugs. Chameleons are even able to change the color of their skin to help them "disappear," or to show if they're feeling angry!

Awesome tongue!!

PACKING PUNCHES

EXPLOSIVE POWER

It's a big, bad, brutal, and savage world out there. Could you ever imagine exploding ants, kangaroos that box, or beetles that squirt chemicals from their butt?

Whether they are packing a powerful punch or mixing up chemicals to make a bomb, these cruel critters are truly awesome. They can use excessive force to get their own way, so stand back and watch these animal antics!

WANNA FIGHT?

Male kangaroos—boomers— get dirty when they fight over a female. They kick out with their massive feet and box with their sharply clawed paws. They are strong enough to crush bone!

Ding ding, round one, and the kangaroo in the blue corner is swinging at the kangaroo in the red corner. Over on the Australian grassland there are two kangaroos battling it out in the boxing ring. It's turning nasty and someone's going to get hurt!

BIG WORD ALERT

MARSUPIAL

say mar-soo-pi-al
An animal that looks after its baby in a pouch.

Kangaroos are part of the marsupial family.

Taking one for the team

This little carpenter ant has given up its life to save the lives of the ants it lives with. When a bigger ant from another nest attacked its home, the carpenter ant exploded its own body, producing toxic yellow glue that killed them both.

Super spit

Spitting cobras can fire blinding venom with a deadly aim. They target their victim's eyes and are accurate 90 percent of the time, even when the victim is moving.

TWIST IT!

Jellyfish can fire their poisoned barbs in under one-millionth of a second!

Never anger a llama—these feisty animals have short tempers and are quick to kick, head-butt, and bite. Freaked-out males also shoot out big gobbets of spit at an enemy!

Ural owls hate to see anyone near their chicks and they lash out with their huge talons, delivering a punch that can knock a man off his feet.

TAKE COVER!

Finding clams is tricky when the crunchy-shelled critters hide in soft mud. Walruses solve the problem by squirting a jet of water to remove the mud, leaving the clams exposed and ready to eat!

A hot shot

This little beetle fears no one because it knows it can fight back using an explosion in its bottom! It keeps two chemicals stashed away near its tail, and when the moment is right they are allowed to mix. The potion gets really hot and explodes, forcing a foul stinging liquid to spray in the direction of an attacker. Impressive!

NIGHT TERRORS

As the sun begins to set, some creatures stir from their sleeping places and prepare for a busy night ahead. Many animals spend the dark time foraging for fruit, berries, and seeds to eat. And while they go about their business, deadly night predators prepare to attack.

In the moonlight, a beastly battle begins as nocturnal creatures fight to survive. With little light to help, animals rely on superb eyesight, or other senses, to find their way in the dark.

There are two types of bat: one type mainly hunts insects, while the other type mainly eats fruit.

DANGER IN THE DARK

Going batty

Bats are one of the most common types of mammal in the world, and masters of the night sky. They have good eyesight, but rely on their senses of hearing and smell to hunt (see Key Facts, below). Just one bat can feast on thousands of flies in a single night. Others are able to grab fish or crabs out of water.

TWIST IT!

Big cats are more successful when they hunt at dawn and dusk. It is cool enough for animals to graze, but it's harder for them to spot a tiger or lion lurking in the dim light.

Scientists used to think tarsiers were silent, but now we know they make lots of sound but it is so high-pitched we can't hear it.

AFTER DARK!

Bats have few predators of their own, so they can live to 20 years of age!

KEY FACTS

Big eyes

Black and white

Big ears

Echolocation

The devil comes out at night!

The forest at night can be a noisy place, and one of the scariest sounds is made by a devil when it's getting mad! Tasmanian devils—tassies—are famous for being grumpy and when they fight over food they growl and screech, and bare their enormous teeth. They have one of the strongest bites in the animal kingdom and hunt snakes, rats, mice, and birds.

If you liked leaping around between branches in the dark, you'd need eyes this big! I'm a tarsier and I chase insects, birds, and lizards at night. If I didn't have amazing eyesight I'd go hungry, or even worse... I'd fall out of the tree!

How gorgeous am I? I'm a red-eyed tree frog. During the day I hide my lovely colors under a leaf but at night I come out to hunt insects. If I get scared I flash my red feet and make my eyes bulge out of my head. Bet you can't do that!

33

DEFEND OR DIE

WE'RE OFF THE MENU!

In most beastly battles there is an attacker and a defender. These careful critters are determined to keep off the lunch menu, but it takes some smart defense tactics to stay alive.

There are some cool weapons on display here, from multi-colored froggy jumpsuits to animal acrobatics. And it's amazing what you can do with some spare bottom-gas!

Squirts blood out of its eyes!

Tears of blood

This short-horned lizard has one of the most bizarre defense mechanisms on Earth—it can shoot blood from its eyes! Some species of short-horned lizard are capable of squirting blood in this way when they feel threatened, by rupturing the tiny blood vessels in their eyelids.

Foaming mess

Grasshoppers can make a perfect snack for birds, but not this one! Foam grasshoppers create clouds of bubbly liquid, which pour out of holes in their skin and become a toxic cloak. The foam smells disgusting and tastes revolting.

Touch me and you'll regret it

Toxic caterpillars have seriously nasty spines.

Some people say I can be a bit prickly at times, but I think my tough outside gives a bad impression. Really, I'm a bit of a softie and I just need to look after myself. My spiny skin helps me hide against a tree trunk but I don't take any chances, and that's why my spines are totally toxic!

What a stink

BELCH!

You think you're so big and clever, but look at what I can do! My gorgeous black and white coat is doing a great job of making sure you notice me, which is good because I can put on one impressive show. Watch me doing a handstand—come nice and close... closer... perfect. Now, I'm going to spray a foul and stinky liquid at you!

TWIST IT!

Froghoppers are high-jumping insects. Their young protect themselves by making foamy nests, called cuckoo spit. They drink lots of plant sap then blow gases out of their bottom to make the foam!

The caterpillars of large white butterflies are great at vomiting, so when they get scared they simply throw up all over an attacker!

Male duck-billed platypuses can lash out with venomous spurs on their hind legs.

Slow lorises are small forest primates. They release toxins from their elbows, which they mix with spit to make a deadly cocktail. Even leopards are scared of them.

STAY AWAY

Polecats spray such a disgusting liquid that they are rarely attacked. Striped polecats can produce ear-splitting screams, too.

Black and white is so last year. We frogs prefer to stay trendy and insist on dressing in the latest must-have jumpsuits in glorious shades. It's not just about fashion of course. Our multi-colored skin screams "poison" at any nasty snakes or brutal birds that fancy a dish of frogs' legs for dinner.

Natty dressers

NATURE'S FOULEST FIVE

Blood-sucker

This marine woodlouse clamps onto the tongue of a fish, then sucks the blood from the fish's tongue until the tongue dies. The creature stays firmly attached in the fish's mouth, working like its original tongue, eating scraps of food, mucus, and blood!

Gut-grower

Tapeworms live inside an animal's gut, surviving on semi-digested food. The hooks on the top of its head keep it securely attached. Tapeworms inside human guts have grown to 37 feet long and can survive for years!

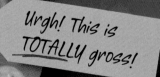

Urgh! This is <u>TOTALLY</u> gross!

Gas attack

This lovely walnut sphinx moth has a nasty habit—when it's scared it passes gas! There's nothing like a bottom burp to keep everyone away!

Baby

Mom!

Monster chick

This chick is not as cute as it looks. It's a young cuckoo and its mother laid her egg in the nest of another bird—dunnocks are common hosts. When the egg hatched, the chick threw the other bird's chicks out of the nest. The poor step-parents then keep feeding the monster chick until it leaves home.

Woah, gas power!

Vile vulture

Turkey vultures usually feast on dying or dead animals. They poop on their own legs to keep cool, and stuff in their poop has the added bonus of killing the nasty bacteria that like to live on their blood-soaked feet.

FAMILY FEUD

FLESH AND BLOOD

Animal battles are not always between predator and prey. Sometimes members of a family or group turn into murderous monsters and attack one another.

Family in-fighting happens when animals want food, to mate, or when bad tempers boil over into brutal behavior.

Get out of my room!

Both male and female cats have territories. They mark their space with smells to tell others to keep out, but if that doesn't work then a fierce fight may follow—these female leopards will settle their score with fangs and claws.

BIG WORD ALERT

TERRITORY

An area or space animals call their own.

Baboons go berserk

Baboons are monkeys that live in large family groups called troops, and they are famous for their family meltdowns! They solve their problems with violence, and as they are fast, fearsome, and fanged they can do a lot of damage.

* Males often chase and attack females, making a loud "wahoo" call to scare them and keep other males away.

* Male baboons sometimes kill baby baboons.

* Males fight with each other to take over a family group and become the troop's "top dog."

Not so gentle giants

Family groups of giraffes are mostly made up of females, but males wander nearby hoping to join the gang at mating time. Sometimes, a fight brews when two males—who may be related—bump into each other. The battle involves head-butting and whacking each other with their necks. It can easily end in death for one of the males.

Watch it!

This looks like a lovely neck-cuddle, but it's actually giraffe-speak for "Get outta here now, before I wallop you!"

TWIST IT!

These are tough times for polar bears. The ice in their cold Arctic home is melting, and it's harder for the giant carnivores to hunt. As a result, they are becoming more likely to turn cannibal and eat polar bear cubs.

Chimpanzees usually eat plants and bugs, but they sometimes get a taste for meat, and attack chimps from neighboring groups. They even eat baby chimps.

Lions don't make good step-dads. When a male lion takes over a new pride he may kill all the cubs. This mean streak works well, as all the lionesses are quickly ready to start a new family with him.

BABY BASHERS

Crazy coots

Coots are waterbirds with a short fuse. If the chicks pester mom or dad for food, the exhausted parents may lose their temper and start to peck back at them. If the hungry chicks don't get the hint, they may be pecked to death. It's common for coots to begin with as many as nine chicks, but end up with only two or three.

EIGHT GREAT DINNER DATES

THE MOST BRUTAL BEASTS

They may be short on good conversation but these brutal beasts have got killer skills that will bring any party to life! We've chosen them as our favorites, some you've met before in this book and some are new—but who would be on your invitation list?

We reckon these are some of the most impressive animals in the world.

DINNER INVITATION

T-REX

Possibly the scariest meat-eater that ever lived, the Tyrannosaurus rex—or Terrible Lizard—was a massive dinosaur. His head alone measured 5 feet long and just look at those saw-edged teeth!

DINNER INVITATION

HONEY BADGER

Honey badgers have a foul temper and are totally fearless. We admire them because they will attack and kill almost anything—that gives them top scores for brutality!

DINNER INVITATION

GIANT OCTOPUS

This Pacific giant octopus is a phenomenal predator and, for an added bonus, it looks like something from outer space! Its weapons are its sucker-covered tentacles, containing 2,240 suckers in total, and a fierce bite.

Diver

DINNER INVITATION

DEATHSTALKER SCORPION

Deathstalker scorpions have a stinging spray of acid, and huge front limbs for crushing their prey—but we've chosen them because they look like mini-monster car-crushers.

DINNER INVITATION

NILE CROCODILE

More dangerous than a great white shark, more cunning than a cobra—the Nile crocodile snaps and grabs. And how many animals do you know that can spend all day pretending to be a log before springing into action?

DINNER INVITATION

KILLER WHALE

Killer whales, or orcas (their correct name), carefully plan their attacks and can work as part of a deadly team. Killer whales hunt and slaughter their prey with ruthless determination.

DINNER INVITATION

SPOTTED HYENA

Horrible hyenas look as if they are enjoying themselves when they go on a killing spree. They cheerfully rip limbs off a body and can crunch bones with their oversized jaws.

DINNER INVITATION

BULLET ANT

If you had to choose between walking on broken glass or holding a handful of bullet ants, we suggest the glass! These tiny terrors have big jaws and their stings burn like nothing else on earth.

WE WANT BLOOD

The thought of drinking blood may be repulsive, but it's the world's best power drink. It's even better than an energy shot, because it's packed not just with energy, but with life-giving ingredients.

Animals that feed on blood have just one big problem—how do they get to the blood? These brutal beasts have discovered some nifty tricks to reach the red stuff.

Pierce and suck

The deadliest of all blood-suckers is the mosquito, because it passes on the killer disease malaria when it feeds. A mosquito has a needle-like mouthpart which it injects into flesh and uses to suck up blood.

Scratch and lick

Vampire bats scrape the skin away from their victim's feet or ankles with their teeth, then lick up the blood. Vampire bats usually prey on horses and cows, but they do sometimes feed on sleeping humans!

How can blood-feeders feed without being discovered by their prey?

They may inject a painkiller into their feeding spot, so the victim can't feel them break the skin, and they may pour a chemical into the wound that keeps the blood flowing quickly.

The all-in-one meal

Blood contains:

95 percent water

Protein—useful for building muscles

Sugar—useful for instant energy

Vitamins and minerals— useful for growing

Blood doesn't contain much fat, so blood-feeders don't have long-term energy stores. That means they must feed often, or starve to death.

Scrape and swallow

Vampire fish swim into another fish's gills and use their needle-like teeth to scrape at a blood vessel until it breaks open. The fish then simply swallow the blood as it pours out.

Peck and sip

Vampire finches enjoy a booby bloody banquet when there is no other food around. They peck at the skin and feathers of a booby (a type of bird) until they draw blood.

Good guy or bad guy?

Oxpeckers are birds that peck blood-filled ticks off the skin of animals, such as antelopes—and that's great for the antelopes who are then pest-free. But oxpeckers like the flavor of these mini-snacks so much they sometimes go one step further, and peck at the blood-soaked wounds left by the ticks, causing the poor animal even more harm and pain.

BLOOD LUST

A tick can increase in size ten times after it has fed.

Vampire bats find their prey by sensing the heat from their bodies, and also by using heat-detectors to find a blood vessel under the victim's skin.

Only female mosquitoes feed on blood. They need it to be able to lay their eggs.

Blood contains a lot of water, so vampire bats must pee while they are feeding to get rid of some of the water, or they'd be too heavy to fly!

TWIST IT!

People kill Amur leopards because they like their fur and turn it into coats. There are only about 30 Amur leopards left alive in the wild. Their home is now protected from poachers, but their future is bleak.

Orangutans live in trees, and when these are cut down they have nowhere to live. The rainforests of Sumatra they have nowhere to live. The rainforests of Sumatra are being destroyed to grow palm oil and there are even plans to build a road through their last habitat.

HUNTED TO DEATH

Humans mainly hunt animals for food and fur. Long ago, we only took what we absolutely needed, and we lived in harmony with the ecosystem. In modern times, we have become greedy.

Rhinos used to roam throughout Africa and Asia. Then people decided (wrongly) that their horns were magical and could cure diseases. Rhinos are killed and their horns cut off to be sold. Western black rhinos were declared extinct in 2011.

EXTINCT!

HOMELESS

An animal's home is its habitat, and when that habitat is destroyed by people—often to plant crops or build roads and homes—the animals have nowhere to live or hunt.

There were about 4,000 South China tigers in the 1950s. Then their forest habitat was destroyed and the big cats were killed as "pests." By the 1990s there were about 50 tigers left and none have been seen in the wild now for 25 years.

EXTINCT?

BRUTAL

IT'S THE END OF THE ROAD...

Animals can be pretty brutal, but maybe the award for the most dangerous product of nature should go to humans.

Since we've been on the planet we have destroyed habitats, hunted entire species to death, and we continue to make our planet a perilous place for the animals we share it with.

ENDANGERED!

The sea lions of the Galapagos Islands live in large groups on rocky shores. Humans have brought new animals, such as dogs, to the islands. These alien invaders carried diseases that killed the sea lions. They can also catch a deadly disease spread by mosquitoes.

ALIEN INVADERS

An animal that has moved into a place it doesn't belong is called an alien invader, and it may upset the ecosystem. Often, it is humans that cause the problem by moving animals around.

EXTINCT!

The dodo was a large flightless bird. When European sailors came to their island home of Mauritius they brought cats, dogs, rats, and pigs with them. The dodos could not defend themselves, or their eggs and chicks, from these predators and they became extinct by about 1700.

KEY FACTS

LIFE IN THE BALANCE

* People who study how animals and plants live together have come up with a handy word to describe the way they need each other: ecosystem (say ee-koh-sist-em).

* An ecosystem is a place, and all the living things in it. They all affect each other, and often exist together in a precious balance. When a new animal or plant comes into an ecosystem it can change that balance in a bad way.

* Your local park or recreation ground is an ecosystem. Imagine a pride of lions leaving their own ecosystem to live in your park—they would cause havoc!

ENDANGERED!

There are fewer than 2,000 Galapagos penguins left in the wild. They are dying because of pollution in their water, and because they get caught in fishermen's nets. Climate change is also damaging their habitat.

DEATH BY DIRT

Climate change and pollution—which is dirt, dirty air, and rubbish—have damaged the habitats of many animals around the world.

EXTINCT!

The little golden toad used to live in a rainforest in Costa Rica, in Central America. It has not been seen since 1989. Its extinction is thought to be the result of pollution and changes in the climate.

ACKNOWLEDGMENTS

COVER (sp) © NHPA/Photoshot, (b/l) © Eric Isselée - iStock.com; **2** (t) Sipa USA/Rex Features; **3** (t) Gerard Lacz/Rex Features, (b) Dave Beaudette; **4** (sp) © NHPA/Photoshot, (b/l) © Photoshot, (b/r) © Florian Andronache - Shutterstock.com; **5** (t/l) © Eric Isselée - iStock.com, (b/l) Jim Zipp/Science Photo Library, (b/c/l) Dave Beaudette, (b/c/r) © John Downer Productions/naturepl.com, (b/r) Professor Nico Smit; **6** (c) © Tony Heald/naturepl.com, (b/l) © NHPA/Photoshot, (b/r) © Roman Sotola - Fotolia.com; **7** (t) © NHPA/Photoshot, (b) Caters News Agency Ltd/Rex Features, (r) © Anup Shah/naturepl.com; **8** (t) © Sergey Uryadnikov - Shutterstock.com, (b) © Ashok Jain/naturepl.com; **8–9** (bgd) © Rafal Olechowski - Shutterstock.com; **9** (b/r) © Hanne & Jens Eriksen/naturepl.com, (b/l) © NHPA/Photoshot, (t/r) Milan Krasula/Solent News/Rex Features, (t/l) © DG Jervis - Shutterstock.com; **10** © NHPA/Photoshot; **11** (t, c) © NHPA/Photoshot, (b) © Photoshot; **12** (t) Gerard Lacz/Rex Features, (b) Alaska Stock Images/National Geographic Stock; **12–13** © Iakov Filimonov - Shutterstock.com, © Kamil Macniak - Shutterstock.com, © Tribalium - Shutterstock.com, © Martan - Shutterstock.com, © stevemart - Shutterstock.com, © Kamil Macniak - Shutterstock.com, © Gary Blakeley - Shutterstock.com, © Aleksei Gurko - Shutterstock.com, © PILart - Shutterstock.com, (bgd) © SongPixels - Shutterstock.com, (l, r) © dencg - Shutterstock.com; **13** (t) Bartlett, Des & Jen/National Geographic Stock, (b) Bournemouth News/Rex Features; **14** (l) © Ryan M. Bolton - Shutterstock.com, (r) © Florian Andronache - Shutterstock.com; **15** (l) Jurgen & Christine Sohns/FLPA, (r) © Tony Heald/naturepl.com, (t/r) Gustavocarra/Creative Commons License; **16** © Luiz Claudio Marigo/naturepl.com; **17** (t) © Oceans-Image/Photoshot, (c) © NHPA/Photoshot, (b) © David Pattyn/naturepl.com; **18** © Pete Oxford/naturepl.com; **19** (b/l) © Robyn Butler - Shutterstock.com, (c/l) © tratong - Shutterstock.com, (t) Tom Murphy/National Geographic Stock, (b/r) Sipa USA/Rex Features, (t/r) Kevin Deacon; **20** © Sergey Gorshkov/naturepl.com; **21** (t/r) © Herbert Kratky - Shutterstock.com, (c/r) Vaclav Silha/Barcroft USA Ltd., (c/l) Newspix/Rex Features; **22** (c) © NHPA/Photoshot, (t) © Josh Anon - Shutterstock.com, (bgd) © STILLFX - Shutterstock.com, (dp) © Glam - Shuttersrock.com; **23** (t) © Alex Hyde/naturepl.com, (c/r) Jim Zipp/Science Photo Library, (b) © NHPA/Photoshot; **24** (sp) © Photoshot, (r) Behavioural Ecology Research Group, Oxford; **25** (t) © DLILLC/Corbis, (b/r) © Andy Rouse/naturepl.com; **26** Gil Wizen; **27** (t) © NHPA/Photoshot, (c) © Martin Dohrn/naturepl.com, (b) Gerard Lacz/Rex Features, (r) © Roger Meerts - Shutterstock.com; **28** (sp) Tim Green; (b/r) Nicky Bay/Science Photo Library; **29** (t) © Alex Hyde/naturepl.com, (c) © Staffan Widstrand/naturepl.com, (b) © Cathy Keifer - Shutterstock.com; **30** Jurgen & Christine Sohns/FLPA; **30–31** (bgd) © Ghenadie - Shutterstock.com; **31** (c, b) © Michael Richards/John Downer/naturepl.com, (t) Mark Moffett/Minden Pictures/FLPA; **32** © Dietmar Nill/naturepl.com; **33** (l) © Bernhard Richter - Shutterstock.com, (r) © Matej Hudovernik - Shutterstock.com, (b) © Dirk Ercken - Shutterstock.com; **34** (c) Dave Beaudette, (b) Piotr Naskrecki/Minden Pictures/National Geographic Stock; **35** (t) © Cathy Keifer - Shutterstock.com, (b/r) © Dirk Ercken - Shutterstock.com, (c) © John Downer Productions/naturepl.com; **36** (b) Professor Nico Smit, (t) Eye Of Science/Science Photo Library; **36–37** © ririro - Shutterstock.com; **37** (t/r) © Andy Sands/naturepl.com, (c) © Melinda Fawwer - Shutterstock.com, (b) © Holly Kuchera - Shutterstock.com; **38** (b) © NHPA/Photoshot; **38–39** (c) © Richard Du Toit/naturepl.com; **39** © NHPA/Photoshot; **40** (t/l) © DM7 - Shutterstock.com, (c/r) Bartlett, Des & Jen/National Geographic Stock, (b/r) © NHPA/Photoshot, (b/l) © Jeff Rotman/naturepl.com; **40–41** (dp) © idea for life - Shutterstock.com, (dp) © JungleOutThere - Shutterstock.com, (dp) © Matthew Cole - Shutterstock.com, (t) © Green Jo - Shutterstock.com, (t/r) © Taigi - Shutterstock.com, © Alex459 - Shutterstock.com, (t/r, b/l) © Gray wall studio - Shutterstock.com; **41** (c) © Hermann Brehm/naturepl.com, (c/l) © Anup Shah/naturepl.com, (r) © Xavier Marchant - Shutterstock.com, (b/r) Gerard Lacz/Rex Features; **42** (b) Michael & Patricia Fogden/Minden Pictures/FLPA, (t) © Sinclair Stammers/naturepl.com; **43** (t/r) Mark Newman/Science Photo Library, (c) © Villiers Steyn - Shutterstock.com, (b/r) © Jim Clare/naturepl.com; **44** (l) © NHPA/Photoshot, (r) © Kjersti Joergensen - Shutterstock.com; **45** (l) © Kjersti Joergensen - Shutterstock.com, (r) © Alfie Photography - Shutterstock.com

Key: t = top, b = bottom, c = center, l = left, r = right, sp = single page, dp = double page, bgd = background

All other photos are from Ripley's Entertainment Inc. All other artwork by Rocket Design (East Anglia) Ltd.

Every attempt has been made to acknowledge correctly and contact copyright holders and we apologize in advance for any unintentional errors or omissions, which will be corrected in future editions.